How To Draw
Prehistoric Animals

by Linda Murray
illustrated by Shi Chen

Library of Congress Cataloging-in-Publication Data

Murray, Linda, (date)
    How to draw prehistoric animals / written by Linda Murray;
illustrated by Shi Chen.
       p.   cm.
    Summary: Step-by-step instructions for drawing dinosaurs and other
prehistoric animals, including the apatosaurus, dimetrodon, and
sauropelta.
    ISBN 0-8167-3287-6 (lib. bdg.)   ISBN 0-8167-3288-4 (pbk.)
    1. Animals, Fossil, in art—Juvenile literature.   2. Drawing—
Technique—Juvenile literature.   [1. Prehistoric animals in art.
2. Dinosaurs in art.   3. Drawing—Technique.]   I. Chen, Shi, 1957-
ill.   II. Title.
NC780.5.M87   1994
743'.6—dc20   93-23058

Watermill Press

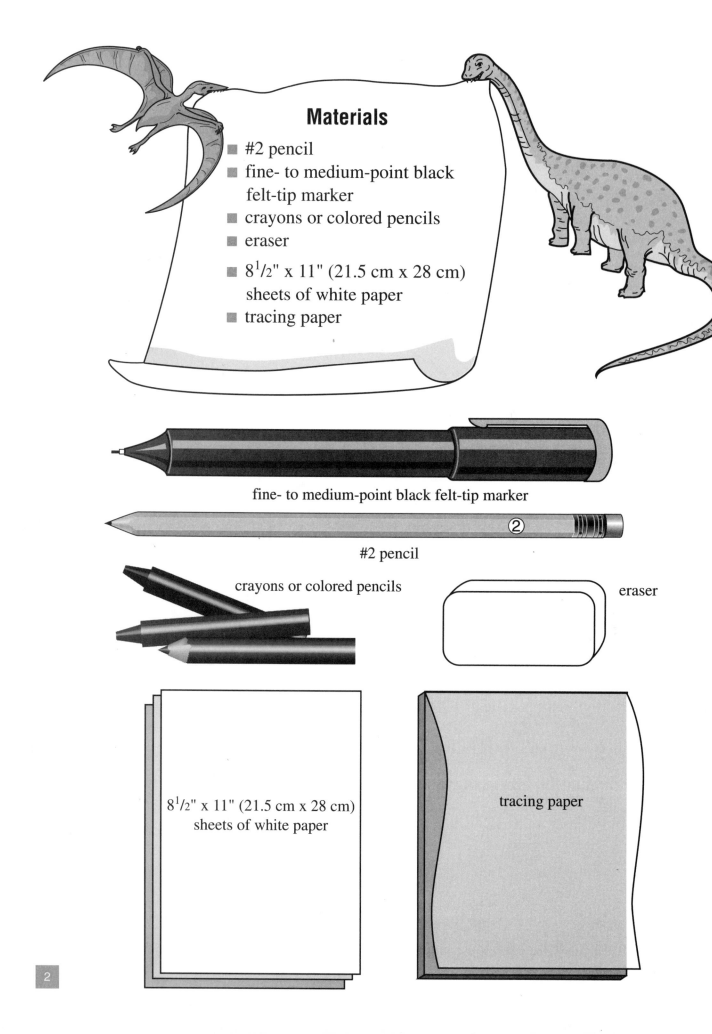

Materials

- #2 pencil
- fine- to medium-point black felt-tip marker
- crayons or colored pencils
- eraser
- 8$\frac{1}{2}$" x 11" (21.5 cm x 28 cm) sheets of white paper
- tracing paper

fine- to medium-point black felt-tip marker

#2 pencil

crayons or colored pencils

eraser

8$\frac{1}{2}$" x 11" (21.5 cm x 28 cm) sheets of white paper

tracing paper

Basic Shapes

You will use only a few basic shapes to draw all the animals in this book:

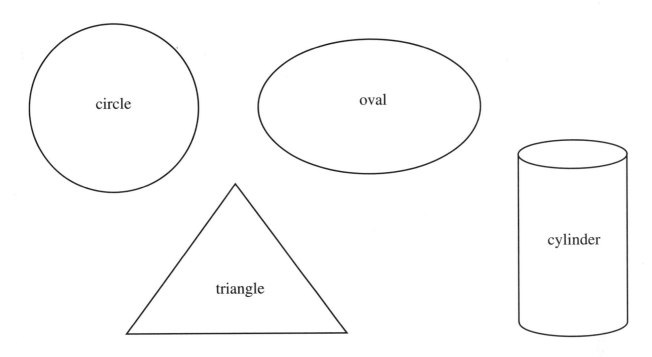

circle

oval

cylinder

triangle

Getting Started

Use the tracing paper to copy the drawings in this book. This will help you when you start to make your own drawings.

Start drawing in pencil, using the basic shapes. Then connect the shapes and add details such as the eyes, nose, and so on. Use the marker to outline the lines you want in your final drawing. Color in the areas you want to highlight, and draw trees, grass, and other interesting things in the background. When you're finished, erase any leftover pencil lines.

It will probably take several tries before you create a drawing you really like. Don't be discouraged if you make mistakes and have to start over. It takes a lot of practice to become an artist!

SALTASAURUS

(salt-uh-SAWR-us)

Saltasaurus had a thick skin covered with bony "plates" which acted like armor to protect it from its ferocious meat-eating cousins. This dinosaur had a very long neck and tail, and could have been 40 feet (12 m) long when it was fully grown.

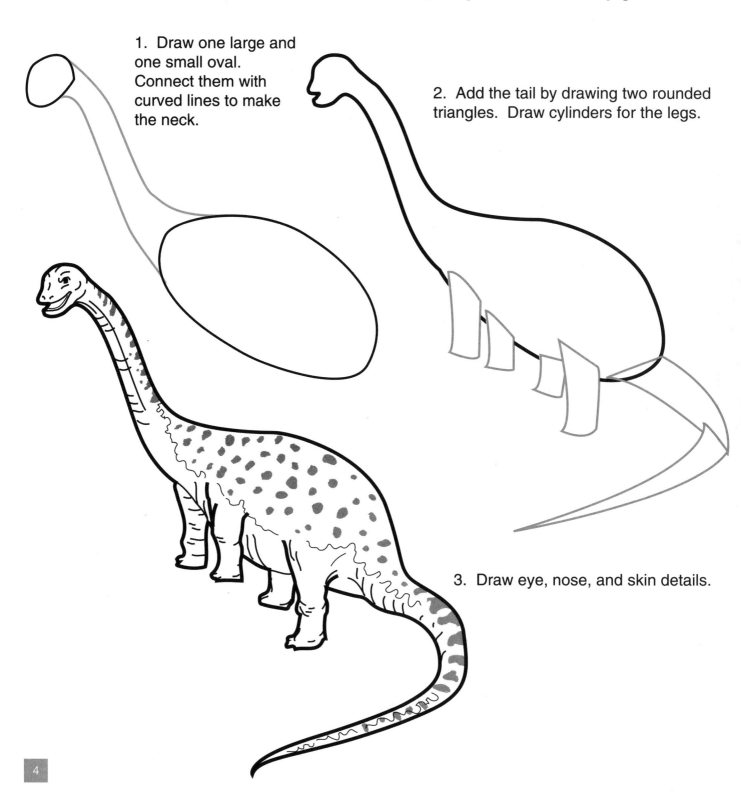

1. Draw one large and one small oval. Connect them with curved lines to make the neck.

2. Add the tail by drawing two rounded triangles. Draw cylinders for the legs.

3. Draw eye, nose, and skin details.

ELASMOSAURUS

(ee-LAZ-muh-sawr-us)

About half of Elasmosaurus' total body length was its neck! This sea reptile would paddle along the surface of the water, hold its long neck up, and look down into the sea. When it spotted food, Elasmosaurus would dive in and scoop it up.

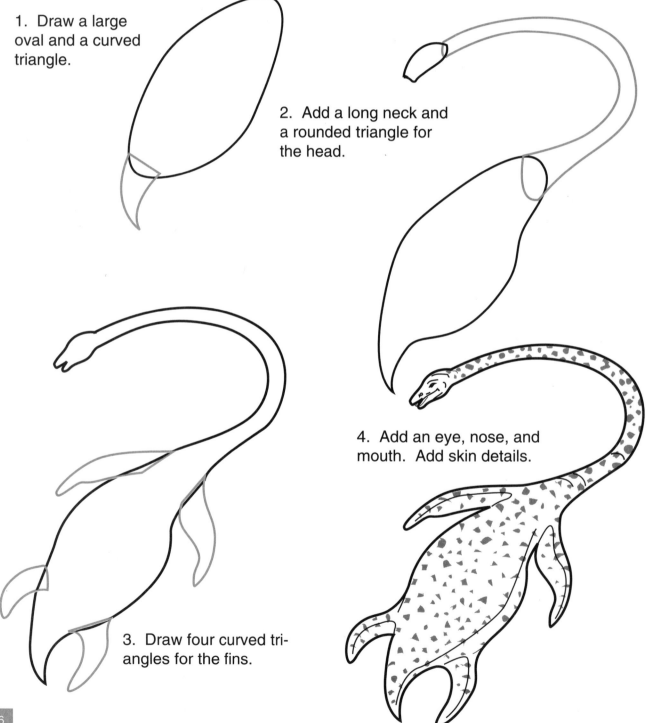

1. Draw a large oval and a curved triangle.

2. Add a long neck and a rounded triangle for the head.

3. Draw four curved triangles for the fins.

4. Add an eye, nose, and mouth. Add skin details.

APATOSAURUS

(ah-PAT-uh-sawr-us)   **also called Brontosaurus**

This dinosaur's name means "thunder lizard," and it's no wonder—Apatosaurus was up to 70 feet (21.3 m) long, and weighed as much as 33 tons (30 metric tons)! Many scientists wonder how Apatosaurus got enough food to eat. It was a plant eater, and probably ate mostly twigs and needles from pine, fir, and sequoia trees. Do you have any ideas?

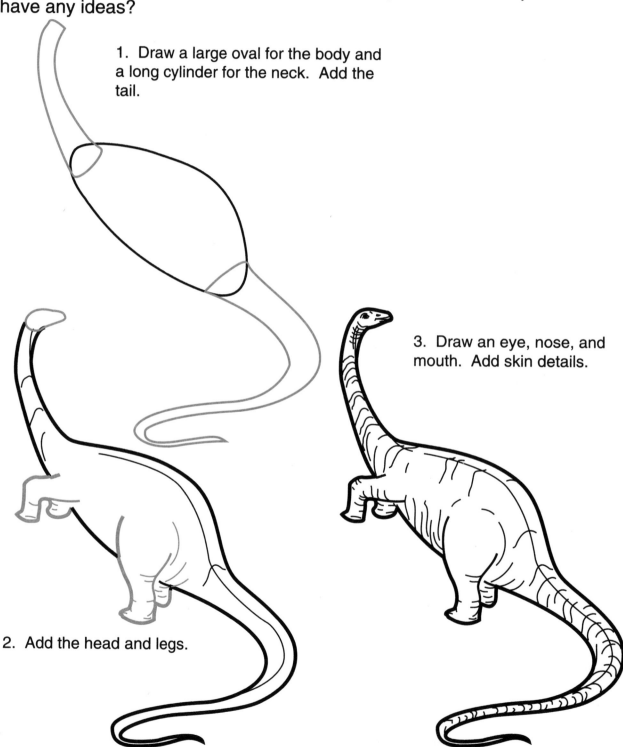

1. Draw a large oval for the body and a long cylinder for the neck. Add the tail.

3. Draw an eye, nose, and mouth. Add skin details.

2. Add the head and legs.

VELOCIRAPTOR

(veh-loss-ih-RAP-tor)

This dinosaur's name means "swift robber." Velociraptor was one of the most feared meat eaters of its time with its sharp, pointed teeth and razor-like claws. Velociraptor was about the size of an adult human, but it could kill animals many times its own size.

1. Draw one large and one small oval. Connect them to make the neck.

2. Add cylinders for the tail, arms, and legs. Draw in the eyes, nose, mouth, and teeth.

3. Add claws and skin details.

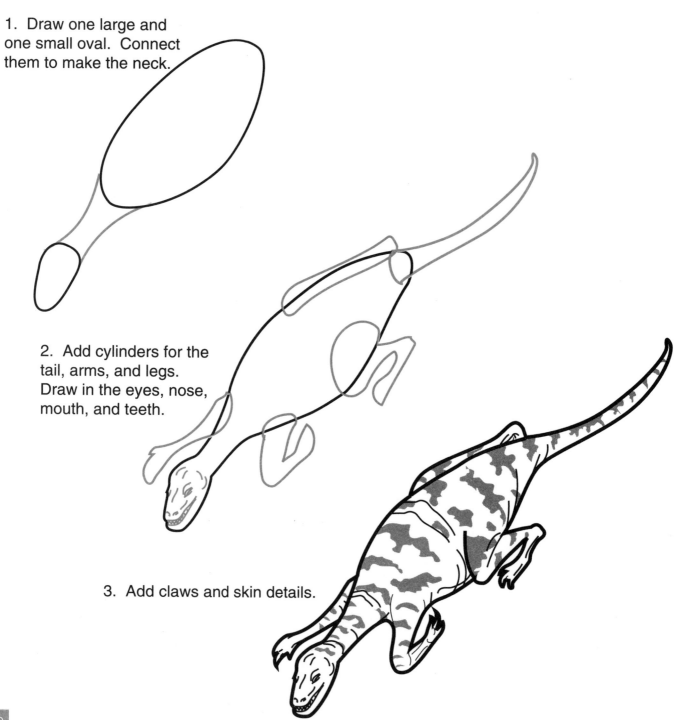

COELUROSAURAVUS

(see-LURE-uh-sawr-A-vus)

This insect-eating reptile glided through the air by means of a flap of skin on each side of its body. It probably lived in the forests. When it wanted to return to land, Coelurosauravus held its legs away from its body to slow its descent. It would have looked like the "flying lizard" that lives today in Southeast Asia.

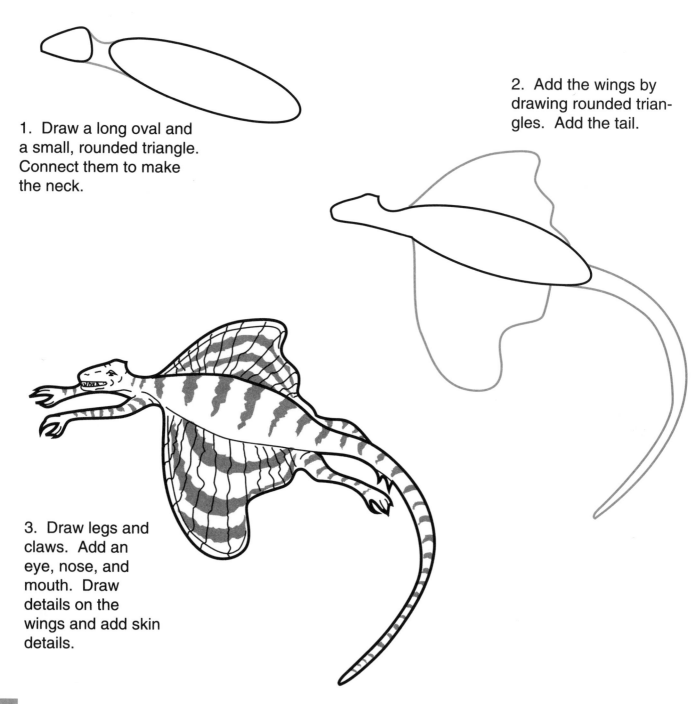

1. Draw a long oval and a small, rounded triangle. Connect them to make the neck.

2. Add the wings by drawing rounded triangles. Add the tail.

3. Draw legs and claws. Add an eye, nose, and mouth. Draw details on the wings and add skin details.

PACHYCEPHALOSAURUS
(pak-ee-SEF-uh-lo-sawr-us)

This plant eater was known as a "dome-headed lizard," or "bonehead." Pachycephalosaurus' skull bone was up to 9 inches (23 cm) thick! Bumps and spikes covered its nose and the back of its head. Pachycephalosaurus probably lived in herds. They were the last survivors of the family of dinosaurs they belonged to.

1. Draw a large oval and a small, rounded triangle. Connect them to make the neck.

2. Add curved cylinders for the tail, arms, and legs.

3. Add claws to the hands and feet. Add an eye, mouth, and "bony" bumps on the head.

4. Add skin details.

STEGOSAURUS

(STEG-uh-sawr-us)

This four-legged plant eater had two rows of bony plates along its back, which it may have used for protection against meat-eating animals. Stegosaurus also had deadly spikes on its tail (some up to 3 feet /1 m long) that could inflict mortal injuries on its attackers. While Stegosaurus was a big animal (20 feet /6 m long), its brain was only the size of a walnut!

1. Draw a large, rounded triangle. Add four cylinders for the legs. Add the head, neck, and the tail.

2. Draw the eye, nose, and mouth.

3. Add feet. Draw spikes on the tail and bony plates along the spine.

4. Add skin details.

PARASAUROLOPHUS
(par-ah-sawr-OL-uh-fus)

The most striking thing about this plant-eating dinosaur was the hollow, hornlike "crest" on top of its head. Parasaurolophus is known as a "duckbilled" dinosaur because the shape of its head and snout resemble a duck. Parasaurolophus' tail is believed to have been brightly colored. The leader would swing its tail to gather the herd.

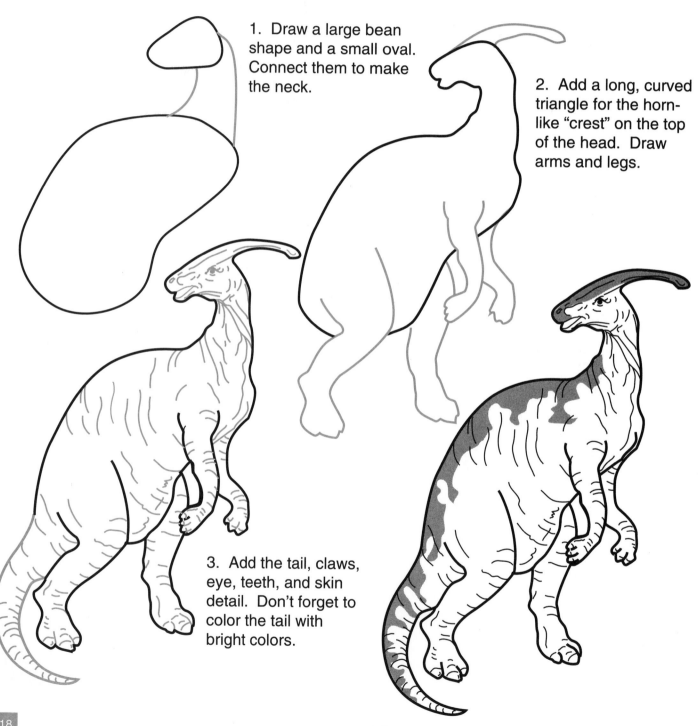

1. Draw a large bean shape and a small oval. Connect them to make the neck.

2. Add a long, curved triangle for the hornlike "crest" on the top of the head. Draw arms and legs.

3. Add the tail, claws, eye, teeth, and skin detail. Don't forget to color the tail with bright colors.

QUETZALCOATLUS

(ket-sol-ko-AT-lus)

This meat-eating, flying reptile was a member of the pterodactyl family, and was probably the largest known flying creature that ever lived. When a fully grown Quetzalcoatlus spread its wings, they were almost 40 feet (12 m) wide from tip to tip! Its wings were made of skin, and attached to its body with a very long "fourth finger."

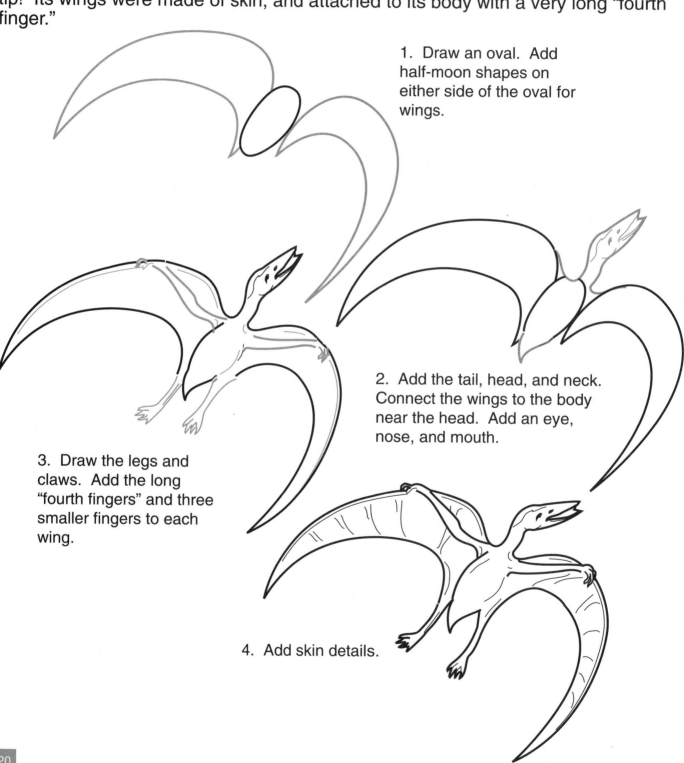

1. Draw an oval. Add half-moon shapes on either side of the oval for wings.

2. Add the tail, head, and neck. Connect the wings to the body near the head. Add an eye, nose, and mouth.

3. Draw the legs and claws. Add the long "fourth fingers" and three smaller fingers to each wing.

4. Add skin details.

OURANOSAURUS

(our-AHN-uh-sawr-us)

This plant eater had a "fin" on its back made from a row of long spines covered with skin. This fin may have helped Ouranosaurus regulate its body temperature. When it wanted to get warm, Ouranosaurus tilted its fin toward the sun. To cool off, Ouranosaurus turned its fin away from the sun.

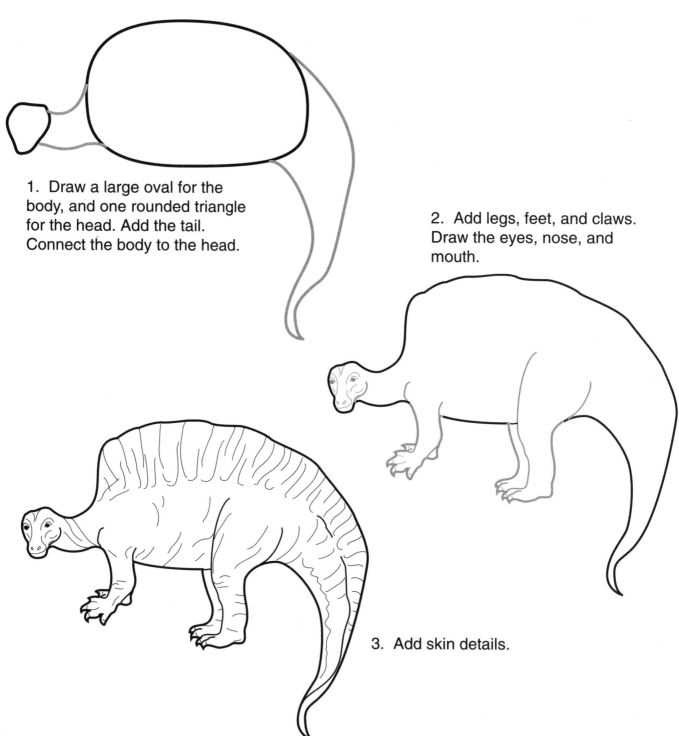

1. Draw a large oval for the body, and one rounded triangle for the head. Add the tail. Connect the body to the head.

2. Add legs, feet, and claws. Draw the eyes, nose, and mouth.

3. Add skin details.

TYRANNOSAURUS
(tye-RAN-uh-sawr-us)

This was the largest, and last, meat-eating dinosaur that ever lived. When fully grown, Tyrannosaurus could have weighed up to 8 tons (7 metric tons)! Tyrannosaurus' arms were only as long as your mom's or dad's, but they were very powerful.

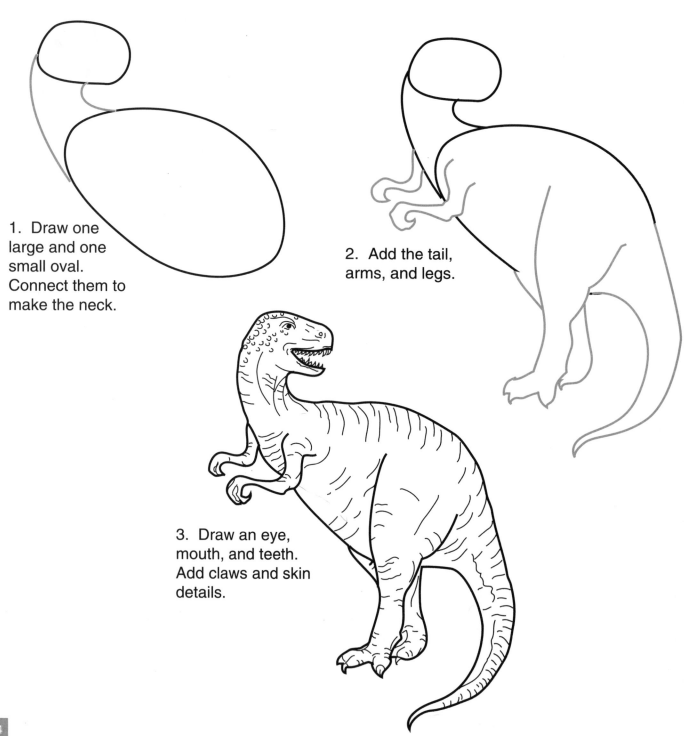

1. Draw one large and one small oval. Connect them to make the neck.

2. Add the tail, arms, and legs.

3. Draw an eye, mouth, and teeth. Add claws and skin details.

TRICERATOPS

(try-SAIR-uh-tops)

Triceratops had a short, thick nose horn and two horns over its eyes, so its name means "three-horned face." The collarlike sheet of bone around this plant eater's neck is called a "frill." Triceratops probably used this frill as a defense shield against meat-eating animals.

1. Draw two ovals and one triangle for the body and head. Add a tail.

2. Add the legs. Draw three horns on the head. Add the eyes and mouth. Draw a wavy line around Triceratops' head to make the bone frill. Draw the nose. Add claws.

3. Add skin details.

SAUROPELTA

(sawr-uh-PEL-tah)

This plant eater's name means "lizard with shield." Looking at Sauropelta, you can see why. Rows of sharp, deadly spikes stuck out from its sides, and it had bone-covered plates running down its back to protect it against predators. Sauropelta looks like a prehistoric tank!

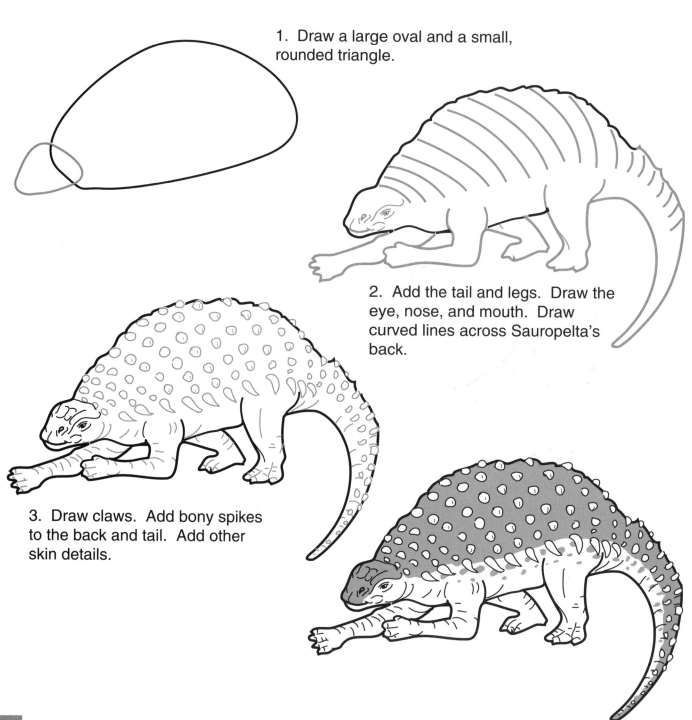

1. Draw a large oval and a small, rounded triangle.

2. Add the tail and legs. Draw the eye, nose, and mouth. Draw curved lines across Sauropelta's back.

3. Draw claws. Add bony spikes to the back and tail. Add other skin details.

DIMETRODON

(dye-MET-ruh-don)

Dimetrodon's name means "two kinds of teeth." It was the largest known meat eater of its time. Dimetrodon was a mammal-like reptile. The huge fin on its back may have controlled Dimetrodon's body temperature by acting like a solar-heating panel.

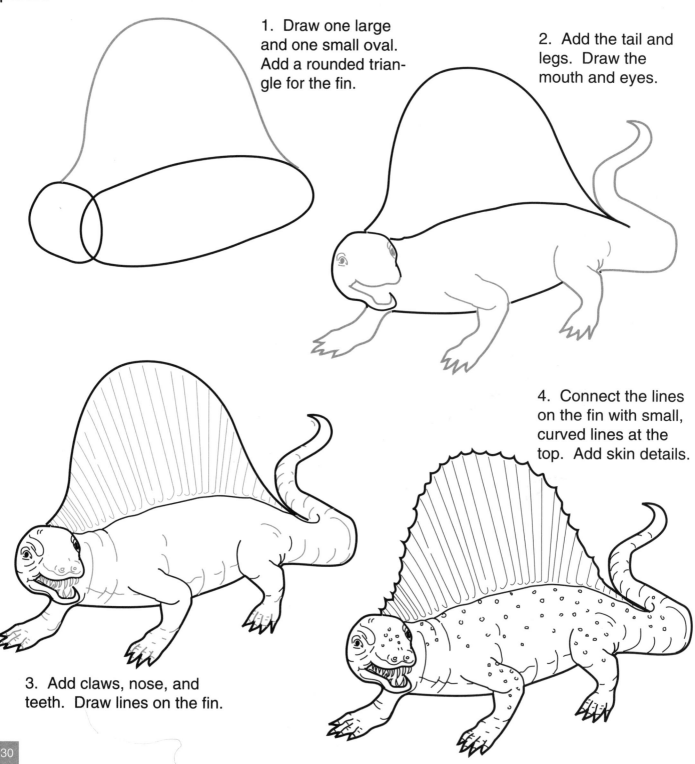

1. Draw one large and one small oval. Add a rounded triangle for the fin.

2. Add the tail and legs. Draw the mouth and eyes.

3. Add claws, nose, and teeth. Draw lines on the fin.

4. Connect the lines on the fin with small, curved lines at the top. Add skin details.